BY INVITATION ONLY

Such is the paradox of café society that many of its components who appear in these pages would, on the whole, prefer to be absent. Many others who have been excluded would prefer to be included in. It must be made clear that some of the more arcane practices described herein apply to the latter grouping, and not the former.

First published by Quartet Books Limited, 1981
A member of the Namara Group
27/29 Goodge Street, London W1P 1FD

Designed by Namara Features and Richard Young

Printed in Great Britain by King's English Bookprinters Ltd, Leeds

BY INVITATION ONLY

Richard Young and Christopher Wilson

QUARTET BOOKS
LONDON   MELBOURNE   NEW YORK

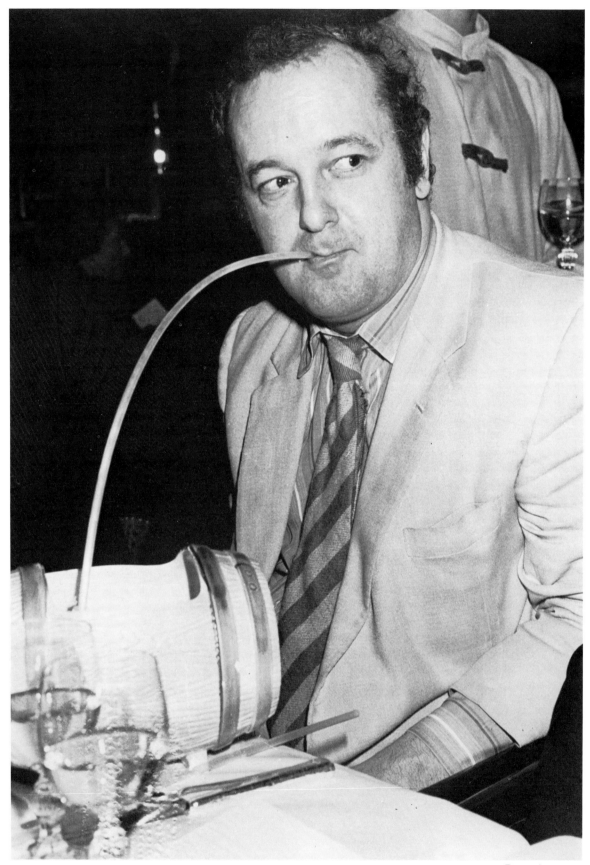

Peter Langan

Foreword

God alone knows why I should introduce you to this book. The people in it veer
between the awesome and the awful. Wilson and Young who wrote it and took the
pictures are the only two people who can grease their way through a door without
opening it. Café society will suffer as a result of its publication. They'll all buy it, and
they'll all condemn it. They'll also all want to take a quick peek in the index to see
whether they're in. I don't want discarded copies cluttering up my restaurant after
they've finished reading it for the 297th time, so I beg you to take it home with you, put it
out on your coffee table, and remind yourselves not to be so silly as to want to take part in
the high life. They're a lovely lot but sometimes they give you the skids, you know.

Peter Langan

Stratton Street
Mayfair W.1.

(scribbled on the back of David Hockney's menu, 26/10/1981)

Photograph by David Bailey, October 1981

RICHARD YOUNG took his first picture of a famous person in 1975, that of Paul Getty Junior, and has never looked back since. He has worked with Cecil Beaton and Ralph Richardson among others and has had his photographs published in newspapers and magazines throughout the world. He has travelled widely and has broadcast interviews for LBC, Capital and BBC Wales. In 1978 ITV made a film about the magazine *Ritz* in which he featured with Frances Lynn and David Lichfield. He has been interviewed in the British Journal of Photography, Tatler, Company, as well as having been portrayed in a three week serial on the life of a social photographer in the *Sunday Mirror*.

CHRISTOPHER WILSON is a Fleet Street journalist who has written for the *Daily Mail*, the *Sunday Telegraph*, the *Daily Express*, the *Times Educational Supplement* and the *Sunday Times*. He also worked for some years for Southern Television as a reporter and presenter. He is thirty-five.

Acknowledgements

I would like to thank Nikon, Leica, Olympus and Canon for making the cameras, Kodak for making the film and Mummy and Daddy for making me; The *Daily Express* and Rex Features for all their help and patience and understanding; Andrew Harvey, picture editor of the *Daily Express* for giving me all the space and freedom to create my own style; Rogers & Cowan, DDA, UK International, Tony Brainsbury and Richard Laver for all their assistance; Stringfellows, Legends, The Embassy, Tokyo Joe's, Wedgies, Regine's and all the clubs around the world that have been wonderful with their assistance and goodwill; the doormen, security people and limousine drivers who have always assisted me in my pursuits; all the record companies for allowing me to gatecrash their parties — (I won't do it again, I promise.) I would like to say a special thank you to Langan's Brasserie, Peter, Richard and Michael for putting up with me; Christopher Wilson for all the hours he has put in; Barry and the team for making the prints; also Derek and Alan for their role in making more prints; to all the newspapers and magazines all over the world that have had to deal with my photographs, John Guiver of National Westminster Bank for all his help and understanding. This book would not have been possible without the help of William Hickey, *Ritz* magazine, Jeffrey Kwintner and Frank Selby.

I would like to dedicate this book to Riitta and the boys for putting up with my late nights and early mornings.

Richard Young

I would like to thank Patrick Stewart, Roy Howard, Ross Benson and Philip Gardner for their various influences and assistances.

Christopher Wilson

"... what a lot of parties ..."

Evelyn Waugh, *Vile Bodies,* 1930

"Give us a mention, love"

Dai Llewellyn to gossip columnist, 1980

It all began with a rather startling piece of news in *The Times*. In the course of a business row with his fellow-directors, the Duke of St Albans returned to his company-owned Rolls-Royce, to find it jacked up minus its wheels so that he couldn't drive it away. He had been sacked.

It was a deeply humiliating moment. His Grace, the tenth of that name and Hereditary Grand Falconer of England, had had his wings clipped. And it started me thinking: if these days they can treat a duke that way, what hope is there for lesser mortals scrabbling their way up the social mountain?

That extraordinary amalgam, Society, is not what it was. The natural pecking-order has changed, and dukes no longer rank in front of marquesses, earls, viscounts and lords. But neither have we reached the American system of animal supremacy where money, and occasionally glamour, mark out your rank.

During the whole of this century, and particularly in the past thirty years, the tumbrils have been rolling for the aristocrats. Some, like the dukes of Devonshire and Westminster, are still glitteringly wealthy and are protected by so much wealth they would need to be followed by several generations of nincompoops and alcoholics to dismantle their fortunes. Others, like the Duke of Marlborough, reign supreme over their serfs in a no-questions asked, feudal style which must make the Queen herself envious indeed.

But for every peer of influence and power, there are now a dozen, two dozen, who have none. Long-lost cousins, lifetime workers in some municipal shrubbery, inherit titles which should have naturally died the death years before. Others, like the Earl of Ypres, end up working as taxi drivers.

This is not to say that Society has disappeared. A glance at the pages of esoteric magazines like *Harpers & Queen*, or *Vogue*, will illuminate the tiny percentage of intermarried and interrelated preserved in aspic, on their perennial social round, away from the limelight, at once proud of their wealth and exclusivity, and at the same time sufficiently ashamed to want to keep away from public view.

This book is not about that dangerously-balanced stratum of society, but about one which is more easily reached. It is the curious joining together of the distinguished and blameless, the well-established, and the frankly upwardly mobile.

On the one hand are former prime ministers, who are prepared to step onto the social merry-go-round. Ranged with them are international celebrities, the true aristocrats, the moguls. On the other, actresses, writers, hairdressers, estate agents, anyone with a cash business – all struggling upwards with their social climbing boots firmly strapped on.

The name is Café Society. The ambition is to have a mantlepiece crammed with those little pasteboard passports which cry out "By Invitation Only".

From the lower end, this curious staging-post can be arrived at through notoriety, sometimes through ill-gotten wealth, always through a determination to outbid and outbeat and outbowl. From the upper, it can be reached by those beyond reproach, in every sense, who make the mistake of mixing with people they don't know.

Of the ambitious, some succeed, others fail. For the rules, like this country's constitution, have never been written. Too much ambition and you're finished. Not enough, and no one will notice you. It's a tricky business.

Some of café society's most outstanding characters have ended up in jail, some die prematurely. Others just go missing, cut loose on a life-raft of drugs or booze or bankruptcy. But these are small prices to pay. Social success is there to be had!

At the very centre of this social ant-heap lies Gossip . . . gossip about the people you know, gossip about the people you would like to know, gossip about the people you were gossiping with an hour before. For the truth is that there are very few friendships to be had out of café society. Acquaintanceships will last for a while until one or other drops out of the limelight. Neutral ground, such as restaurants and night clubs, tends to be the natural habitat since many do not want to reveal as much of themselves as would be exposed were they to entertain at home.

If this sounds a chilling indictment, the social mountaineers themselves are quite without qualms.

They deck themselves out and fly to the nearest party, given by an art gallery or a film company or a perfumier. The champagne is never-ending: it is the only drink, we all reassure ourselves. At the Dorchester, a cigar company throws a party for a thousand guests and vintage champagne is liberally poured down eager throats. Round the corner at Les Ambassadeurs, an international jeweller rounds up minor royalty (hopeful of a free sample?) and displays his wares to the accompaniment of a barrage of popping champagne corks.

Another jeweller, not to be outdone, ferries guests to Paris on private jets where a beaker of vintage Krug is in your hand before the seat-belt is clipped together. On arrival by motorcade you find the Place Vendôme marqueed over and the Krug still flowing. If it's not Krug, then it's Roederer, or Bollinger, or Pol Roger or Perignon. A casino is opened underneath the Ritz Hotel. A champagne fountain is erected and started with the flash of a sabre slicing the top from the magnum.

Rarely here is a thought spared for recession, unemployment, the collective future, the individual future, or indeed any future beyond the next glass of champagne.

The essence of this ersatz society is to have fun. And while the delirium created reminds one never so much as that of the pre-Depression desperation of the

1

Thirties, the components of café society have changed.

Few indeed now are the grand hostesses left in London. The Emerald Cunards and Sybil Colefaxes of this world have melted into the ether, to be replaced by the corporate host. Such hostess figures that are left, like Lord Duveen's daughter Dolly Burns, entertain discreetly, if still lavishly, behind closed doors.

Now many of the party-givers have something to sell: themselves, or their products. In the hope of future co-operation from their guests, ungrudging and unstinting comes the hospitality.

And what sort of parties? The ultimate vulgarity of a twenty-five-hour Bacchanalian bonanza to celebrate a quarter-century of the *Playboy* bunny-girl being introduced into this country where guests came clad in few clothes and left with less?

Or the elegant, tented sham of a black-and-gold evening where the widow and mother of socialist peers entertains her international jet-set guests mingling with the aristocrats, the literocrats?

Or the opening party for a Mayfair jeweller, whose guests come winging their way from all over London in hope of free gifts, only to be shamed by their cheapness and tawdriness?

Each, in its way, is a delightful occasion which is enjoyed by the guests and

remembered with affection until the next party. Each, in its way, also leaves the slightly sour taste of saccharin, of an underlying uneasiness about it.

For the guests are never quite sure.

What of the week-long party clubowner Regine gave for a Boeing 707-full of freeloaders who flew to inspect her nightclub in Marbella, only to discover all there was to see was a building site?

Or the teeth-gritting party given by the Duchess of Devonshire at stately Chatsworth to promote a shotgun where a barrel-load of hopeless and dangerous journalists were allowed to pepper off cartridges all day long?

Or the six hundred who turned up to fashion person Percy Savage's party to celebrate something or another, all wearing red?

Some parties given by the ambitious tend to create the opposite to the desired effect. Fanny Cradock, the one-time television cook, is an unfortunate example. On

3

one occasion, a little man sitting in the corner waited patiently until his hostess arrived, then stood up and introduced himself as a representative of the Inland Revenue. He duly handed the hapless Mrs Cradock a writ for unpaid tax, and departed. One guest was asked afterwards what had been Mrs Cradock's reaction to the writ. "I couldn't tell," was the reply, "under all that make-up."

On another occasion, also a Cradock publishing party, she turned up with a huge white satin bow in her hair. "What funny waitresses they have around here," a debby voice shrieked loudly.

There is, mercifully, still some style left. When former Washington Ambassador Lord Harlech celebrated his sixtieth birthday, his American-born wife had half-a-dozen apple trees hacked down to decorate their resplendent Kensington home. Unlike the debutante mother who imported a single tree from South Africa, this was considered extremely chic.

4

5

6

7

8

9

On the other hand, bad taste still prevails. For example, when Bianca Jagger celebrated her twenty-seventh, or thirty-second, or thirty-eighth birthday, depending on which way you look at it and whose version you prefer to believe, she rode a white stallion into the discotheque where the party was being held. Needless to say, the cost of such extravagance did not fall to her: New York frock designer Halston picked up the bill for the 1 a.m. to 7 a.m. bash.

One of the most memorable parties in recent years was in celebration of the Marquess of Blandford, heir to the Duke of Marlborough. To signal his twenty-first birthday, "Sunny" Marlborough invited twelve hundred guests to a dusk-till-dawn

10

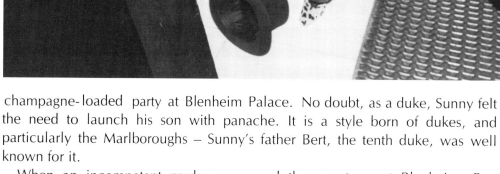

11

champagne-loaded party at Blenheim Palace. No doubt, as a duke, Sunny felt the need to launch his son with panache. It is a style born of dukes, and particularly the Marlboroughs – Sunny's father Bert, the tenth duke, was well known for it.

When an incompetent gardener savaged the rose-trees at Blenheim, Bert refused to sack him – he merely set his dogs on him. On an earlier occasion, while entertaining the late Randolph Churchill, a particularly poor dinner had been served. At last a great silver trolley was brought up and the famished Randolph waited expectantly while the lid was rolled back. In the trolley was Bert's television set, and he contentedly sat back to watch the latest episode of Coronation Street.

It is also Bert who is alleged to have provided the legendary answer to an ill-mannered dinner-guest. As the liveried flunkeys hovered behind each of the score of guests, an American woman turned to Bert and said: "Duke, do you mind if I smoke between courses? It's my little vice." Without batting an eyelid, Bert replied: "Madam, fucking is mine. But I don't do it at the dinner table."

But, to return to the parties, no single individual has managed to repeat the grandeur of entertainment offered by various Government agencies. Outstanding amongst them is the one given by Cable and Wireless, the state-owned company,

14

held at St James's Palace with the Queen as their guest of honour. Nearly two hundred of the seven hundred guests had been flown, all expenses paid, from such exotic places as Ascension Island, Bolivia, Fiji, Haiti, Nepal and the Seychelles. It cost £150,000.

To prove that all is illusion in café society, consider the example of oil heiress Olga Deterding, the supposedly fabulously wealthy eccentric who dominated many a London party until her unfortunate death on New Year's Eve, 1979.

She was the Shell heiress, the uncountably wealthy woman who would have spent all her money on her boyfriends (Alan Whicker, Jonathan Routh, etc.) if only she'd felt like it.

Eccentric she was: she once sat for a whole afternoon in Langan's Brasserie near the Ritz Hotel with no clothes on. She used to run up her own flag from her Piccadilly penthouse "so that friends can see whether I'm in", and she once said she had bought a pair of powerful binoculars so that she could peer from her balcony into the dining-room of the Ritz. "If I see someone there I know with his mistress, I dial down to the restaurant and ask to speak to him saying it is his wife."

She had stuffed sheep ornamenting her penthouse, and used to scatter raisins under them in place of droppings: and she was known to dress up as a waitress at her own parties. But for all the razzmatazz about Olga's legendary wealth, there was very little evidence of it. Her clothes generally were poor – she occasionally looked as though she needed a wash and brush-up – and her drinking, just before she died, led to more than one embarrassing event.

In the end, she died raising her glass to the New Year in an obscure Mayfair drinking club with none of her well-known jet-set friends about her. She choked on a piece of meat. At the time she had 345 milligrammes of alcohol per 100 millilitres of her blood – more than four times the legal limit for drinking and driving. The final irony was that a copy of her will was found on a restaurant floor by a couple of waiters as they swept up just a month later at Meridiana, in South Kensington.

Of course, the parties would be nothing without their guests – and their gatecrashers.

Top of the pile of mainly ex-public school bucks who have had their bottoms kicked out of every major front door in London is Gordonstoun-educated oaf Jeremy Browne who has probably spilt more blood in the pursuit of happiness than a ward-full of blood donors.

Browne's early attempts at gatecrashing parties have raised what was once (and still is) an unpleasant and antisocial act into a peculiar art form.

An early example was the Duke of Fife's dance for his daughter, Lady Alexandra Carnegie, at the RAC Club in Pall Mall. Browne scaled up six floors and managed to get in through a window, only later to be shown the front door. An accomplice fell two floors, cutting himself and ruining his dinner jacket. He still got in.

On another occasion, police and ambulances had to be called to a party given by Sir Geoffrey Vavasour and businessmen Michael Bower for their debutante daughters. Browne and another accomplice had got in and been thrown out. He responded by putting his head through the glass in the front door and ripping the top of a girl's dress away.

15

16

17

18

19

20

21

22

23

Blacklists, Dobermann pinschers at the gates and other security measures seem to have no effect.

Old Etonian Richard Miller crashed a ball at the Café Royal by scaling the outside of the building using a ladder and a window-cleaner's cradle. Two of his friends practised in the art of rock climbing came in through the skylight, using knotted curtains in their efforts to get at the booze.

These, of course, are isolated incidents, even if gatecrashing has become more respectable. But the most outstanding example of gatecrashing, which must surely set a world record, took place at a party at Christie's, the fine-art auctioneers, in 1978. About seven hundred and fifty guests had been invited to a charity auction of Coco Chanel's personal garments. A mass stampede of gatecrashers actually doubled the number of guests. Director John Herbert moans: "There must have been fifteen hundred present, of which only half had been invited. We couldn't keep them out because it was a public auction and by law we're not allowed to turn anyone away." It cost the auction house more than five hundred bottles of champagne.

Set at arm's length away from café society are the Royal Family – or, to the socially ambitious, those members of the Royal Family who are accessible. For in these days of post-regal euphoria there is apparently still a lot to be had from close contact with the Royals.

25

This may seem mystifying to the majority who see the monarchy in the context of duty and figurehead; but there are still a remarkable number of socialites in London who would crawl over their best friend's dead body to receive a royal invitation.

Getting alongside some members of the Royal Family is extraordinarily easy. Others tend not to go out into the world quite so much.

Generally, the easiest way to come into close contact with the Royal Family when you are without background and newly come into money is to join a charity. Those who are acute enough will spot their ideal Royal, look up the charities list, and see which ones that Royal is president or patron of. Then they will join with a modest donation and offers of help. The help may not be forthcoming but the donations increase until the charity finds they are helpless without you. It is at this point you are elected to the committee, and then the introductions begin. The Royal Family get some of their greatest laughs out of meetings with their charities, watching the social climbers try to achieve the impossible: to create a friendship with a Royal.

Some are more approachable than others. Princess Michael of Kent – until Diana Spencer the glamour-puss of the House of Windsor – started a new tradition of moving among the people when she married her Army officer husband. This policy decision was brought about for two reasons. First, her world until her

26

27

29

30

31

32

33

marriage to Prince Michael had been nowhere near royal and, though ambitious herself, she was happier in the company of people one step down the social scale. And secondly, the Queen's refusal to give the Michaels a Civil List expense account meant that their income was restricted: at one stage Michael was earning hardly more than a tube-train driver on overtime.

This meant, in the words of one cynic, "the Michaels would go anywhere for a hot dinner". She social, he willing to be led, they would turn up at quite extraordinary functions not previously associated with royal patronage. Commercial enterprises benefited from her interest, and in her private campaign to get her husband on the Civil List, she let it become known that she was taking dresses from couturiers at knock-down prices; or that she was borrowing them; or, as one Paris couturier revealed, she was being given them.

The campaign failed, and the Princess gave in with good grace, still frantically attending more events than Princess Margaret and Princess Anne put together.

In all these ways, more and more people were being accorded a royal introduction. Other, Civil-Listed members were less easy to get to grips with. The charity-ball queens are Princess Anne, Princess Margaret, the Duchess of Gloucester and Princess Alexandra. But undoubtedly the catch of the year is going to be the new Princess of Wales. Predatory matrons have been sizing her up since her engagement to Prince Charles was announced, and she will have her work cut out keeping away from the climbers.

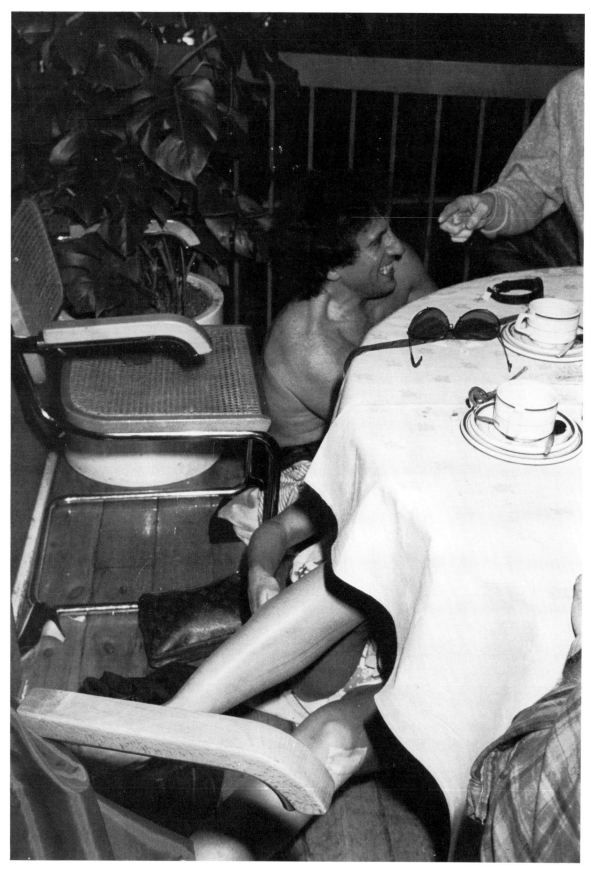

Others, less romantically inclined towards the Royal Family, can have their moments of fun. with the Royals: mercifully, the traffic is not all one-way. Whoever manipulated Princess Margaret into the humiliation of publicly playing bingo in the name of charity must cherish that moment.

Joan Collins is one of the most durable café society figures, usually shadowed around by her sleek and rather self-satisfied husband, Ron Kass. Despite proving her real ability as an actress in her stage play *The Last of Mrs Cheyney* she is still regarded rather humourously by those who happily mix with her at party after party. This unfair judgement stems from her ill-considered autobiography, naming her lovers across the years; her two box-office hits, *The Stud* and *The Bitch* – written by sister Jackie – in which she got to take her clothes off at a rather advanced age (she is now forty-six); and her determination to fudge the issue of how old she really is. In fact, she looks a good ten years younger and is a shining example of how to stay post-menopausally sexy. Her business interests – here, Joan Collins mannequin; there, the Joan Collins jeans – mean that she is one of the very few British actresses who can afford to live like a star.

One of the most disarmingly charming figures around is television personality Russell Harty, who came late into life as a performer on the small screen. Son of a market trader from Yorkshire, he has the bewildered air of someone who has just stumbled across café society and isn't quite sure what to make of it. In fact this is a shrewd device to draw people out, something which in an exaggerated form he

38

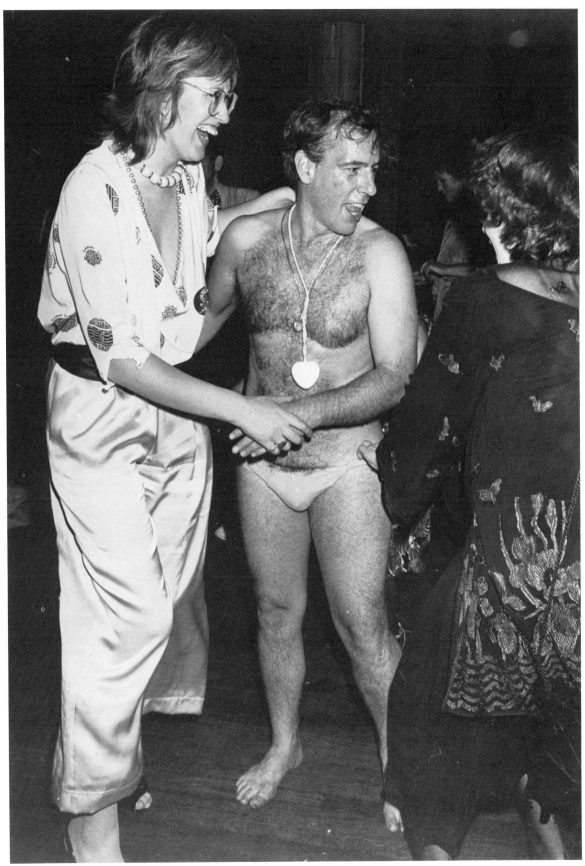

39

uses to good effect on his television interviewees – though sympathy was not all on his side when black pop singer Grace Jones, rather the worse for wear, took a swipe at him on camera. A bachelor, he is remarkably reticent about his private life and, one suspects, would be happier holding down an academic or literary post than flaunting himself before the public.

Undoubtedly one of the richest, fastest and least conventional aristocrats around is Michael Pearson, the heir to Viscount Cowdray and a massive fortune which has never accurately been assessed in print but which includes estates, the famous Cowdray Park polo ground, Lazard's merchant bank, the *Financial Times* and a long string of provincial newspapers – and also Château Latour, the most delectable claret known to civilized man. However, he spends much of his time, like other scions of the titled Earl Jermyn and the Earl of Rocksavage, in tax exile in Monte Carlo with his German-born wife, Fritzi. Vicki Hodge, the daughter of baronet Sir John Hodge, comes from that same period and had an amazingly long career as a model. She is perhaps best known for her long-standing relationship with tough-guy "actor" John Bindon, who successfully pleaded not guilty to murdering gangland figure John Darke after a disagreement at the amusingly named Ranelagh Yacht Club in Fulham (they do not send representatives to Cowes and there are precious few boats with that name on the stern). Far from his acting

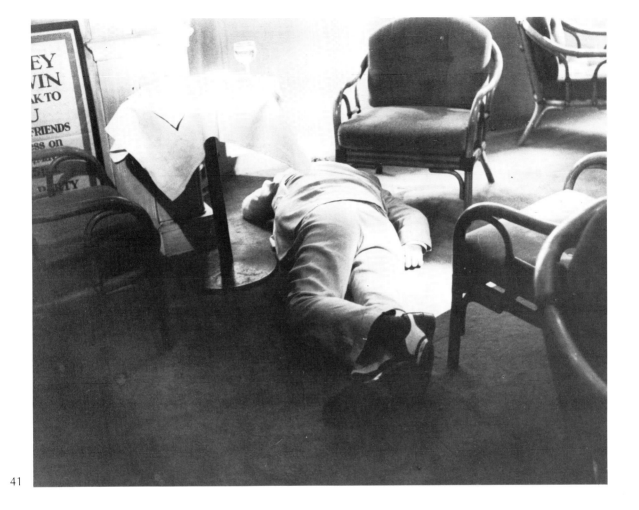

41

talents, Bindon rose to fame in café society for being able to do a trick about his person with half-a-dozen beer mugs. Despite this enormous talent, Vicki left him recently.

To millions of pin-up fans, Marilyn Cole represents Woman personified: heavy-breasted, regular features, from a background not dissimilar to their own and yet the Girl Who Made It. From shopgirl at a Co-op in Portsmouth to Britain's first *Playboy* centre-spread is a huge leap, and one which she achieved with ease. Now she was squired by the likes of Baron Steven Bentinck, Sir William Pigott-Brown, and ex-Playboy chief, Victor Lownes. Acquaintances, however, still refer to her unkindly and behind her back as "Co-Op"; it seems she is Goddess only when she is between the sheets of *Playboy* magazine.

Anthea Redfern is the girl who perfected the marital trick of Having Your Cake and Eating It. After separating from the egregious Bruce Forsyth and whisking round town with an unmemorable figure called The Plank, presumably for obvious reasons, she returned to the family fold where she and Brucie now live. However, it has never been made clear whether this is a Reconciliation or merely Convenience: they are not seen out and about together very much.

Zandra Rhodes, apart from being one of our most talented fashion designers in generations, is also much taken by the opposite sex. In a moment of proclivity she

allowed a young man to attach himself to her, by name Eric Douglas. Douglas, the precocious son of Kirk Douglas, had come to London to study and immediately put himself up at the Dorchester Hotel. "Where else," inquired the little whipper-snapper, "can one get clean linen and room service for £70 a week?" This figure is slightly misleading: full board at the Dorchester at the time cost a minimum of £525.

Emerging, chrysalis-like, from the corridors of power, Lady Falkender has made a suprising hit amongst café society. Under Sir Harold Wilson she had wielded so much power in Downing Street that she was labelled the First Woman Prime Minister of Britain. The transition to figure of fashion is something which she clearly enjoys, whether locking herself in the ladies' loo at Langan's Brasserie while the owner bellowed to be let in, or on her more sedate trips around town with her walker, dentist Mark Gilbert. Despite being a political animal, Marcia Falkender still has to make her maiden speech in the House of Lords, seven years after she was conferred her peerage by a grateful Wilson. Still surprisingly sexy at age forty-nine.

Enjoying the status of celebrity his sudden retirement from *News At Ten* brought him, Reggie Bosanquet has emerged as a darling of society guest-lists. Indeed, such is his status now that he represented Britain in a £1 million star-studded party in Paris, with guests from all over the world. It was Reggie's Rolls-Royce that spearheaded a huge motorcade across Paris, though one has to add that Reggie

43

found the proceedings so tiresome he returned to the Rolls and slept in the back of it until it was time to go home. Not best known for a consistent sense of humour: when gossip columnists raided his room while staying with Playboy chief Victor Lownes, he chased them, toupée-less, down the corridor, uttering shocking threats.

The joke goes that since Edward Fox played the Duke of Windsor in the television series *Edward and Mrs Simpson* he has at last found a character for himself: long after the series was over, the wardrobe and the mannerisms remained. He is not above the irony of the situation: when he gave a party for his blonde and pert daughter Lucy, the invitations went out from "Edward and Mrs Simpson" – his ex-wife Tracey Reed (Lucy's mother) is married to actor Bill Simpson.

Thankfully, there are those left in café society who combine dilettantism with a certain style. They are few and far between, but one outstanding example is Blue Star Garages heir and Old Harrovian Rupert Deen.

Here is a day in his London life: "I get up at 9.30. I go out and buy the newspapers. I get the *Mail,* the *Express,* the *Sporting Life,*and the *Financial Times.* Next, I have a bath, between eleven and twelve as I complete my levée, I phone

44

45

my friends. I might do a bit of business phoning too, about horses or insurance."
Apart from that, not much. Like Olga Deterding in her day, Rupert does not work.
He is not an enthusiastic supporter of female suffrage, but is warmer towards
apartheid. He collects bears, and spends an inordinate amount of time in the aptly
named Drones in Pont Street. His friends include what was known to some as the
Drones' Set: Michael Pearson, John Bentley, Minah Bird, and various others.
Together, they are represented in an oil painting in Tokyo Joe's, the Piccadilly
nightclub – no doubt in the hope they will one day go there and spend some of
their collective millions.

Love affairs come and go in café society like waiters through the swing doors. It
has become less fashionable for the multi-marriage, pioneered by such as the Earl
of Kimberley, who has attached himself to so many different wenches over the
years that "Countess of Kimberley" is rapidly becoming a more common name
than, say, Mary Smith.

Since café society is cross-pollinating in much the same way as *Debrett* carries
the names of famous families over and over again in its pages, it becomes quite an
amusing pre-dinner trick to work out the various chains of association: "Well, Jane
was with Jonathan, he'd had Juliet who was with George for a time, who used to
be with Gemma who had a stand with Jason who *lived* with Jane."

Of course, since the huge increase of bisexuality amongst the chic and cheerful,
these kinds of chain-relationships have become a lot more complicated and

nowadays involve more and more people.

The associations are carried aloft by most on a cloud of champagne and by many on a cushion of assorted drugs. The most popular of these in the past five years has been cocaine – the "social drug". The thrill of cocaine for its users goes far beyond the high achieved via a quick snort up the nostrils. It is highly illegal and those caught in possession can be accused of trafficking if they carry more than a certain amount around. Mere possession of a narcotic in general, carries a fine; it is considered socially acceptable to be caught under these circumstances. A trafficking, or pushing, offence is a different matter altogether. But the thrill is in handling a narcotic, a "dangerous" drug.

Of course, cocaine *is* dangerous – for different people in different ways. The oft-described "sporting baronet" – he was once a champion amateur jockey – Sir William Pigott-Brown discovered one way when he went on a trip to South Africa with newspaper magnate Lord Rothermere's nephew Esmond Cooper-Key and others.

He was arrested after a bottle of cocaine was found in his jacket while he was staying in Capetown. In fact, he said, the cocaine had been given to him by the Prince of Bhutan while they were bear hunting and he developed toothache: the Cape Town magistrates found this a perfectly reasonable explanation and acquitted him.

But the very possession of the substance turned out to be hazardous.

Its danger to others is more damaging. Amongst café society you will see young men whose faces are set in hard lines, whose youth is dissipated and whose devil-may-care attitudes in the clubs and restaurants are all too predictable: these are the prematurely aged no-hopers who have taken indulgence just that bit too far. One young man I knew whose riches were breathtaking, grew old in his twenties. In two years he went from a bouncing, witty, amusing man with a string of cars and a string of girls, to the picture of a clapped-out boxer, with wary eyes, a constant sniff and an indifferent future in front of him.

What is astonishing is the audacity with which these drugs are taken. In many of the major clubs and restaurants I have been into in London and New York, drugs are being taken to improve the shining hour.

Even the most respectable nightclubs are used for drug-taking, though it must be said, clandestinely and without the owners' knowledge. Take, for instance, one in Jermyn Street. Any night of the week you will find the closets in the men's and ladies' loos containing not one, but often a number of people. There is nothing sexual about their incarceration: they are taking a "toot".

I once saw a close friend of some of the Royal Family after a party at the Ritz taking a toot in the foyer. Had any of the staff seen, he would have been ejected or arrested. Fortunately his ludicrous exhibitionism went unnoticed.

49

50

51

53

There is a hideous cocktail of other drugs which can be taken in any number of permutations: amyl nitrate, amyl sulphate, methedrine, benzedrine, quaaludes, angel dust (a horse tranquillizer), green (child anaesthetic), ether cocktails, acid and, at the top of the tree, heroin. For the brave few, heroin is injected, for the merely foolhardy, it is sniffed in powder form, sometimes being mixed with cocaine.

The use of these drugs is extensive and indiscriminate: there is always a hardy handful of members of café society who would like to try everything at least once.

The most lowly drug, still familiar and still popular, is marijuana, which most people consider socially perfectly acceptable in any circumstances, even though it is actually illegal.

No better example can be given of how its use may potentially ruin a conventional social situation than when the Countess Mountbatten held a party in Knightsbridge which was attended by the Queen and Prince Philip. Unknown to Lady Mountbatten and her husband Lord Brabourne –let alone the Queen – young guests came out of the party to sit on the pavement and smoke "joints". Their behaviour was rowdy and outrageous. Fortunately, they had the sense to clear out of the way, picking up their shoes as they left, before the Queen re-emerged.

Why this extraordinary search for oblivion? Café society is, by and large, made up of individuals who are rich, talented, good-looking and outgoing. They

55

instinctively find each other, gravitate towards each other, and mingle. They may not have more than one of these characteristics, there are an awful lot of ugly people about; but somehow they qualify.

Perhaps there is not enough to struggle for, and by flouting the law they offer themselves some kind of challenge. Perhaps oblivion is always preferable to reality because it puts off thoughts of the long term, thoughts of the day when the café doors will be shut. Other values which members of day-to-day society have — hard work, relative sobriety, family life and planning for the future — do not figure in these people's lives.

And the shame that is attached to high-born families, such as the Duke of Devonshire's and Princess Margaret's friend Colin Tennant's, when their children are discovered to be under the influence of heroin, is as great as that of the back-street mother who discovers her teenager sniffing a glue-bag. Same problem, different circumstances.

That is one end of the scale of café society. At the other, aiming towards it like a car sailing towards its inevitable ultimate smash, is something still relatively fresh; the debutante season.

At the beginning of February each year, socially ambitious mothers band together for a series of lunches which will result, they always fantasize, in the

62

56

next-generation-but-one being assured for all.

Despite all the denials, the debutante season is still a marriage market *par excellence*, and while heirs to stately homes will occasionally start at this stage to express their preferences for their own sex rather than the opposite, and while girls with tidy fortunes will show a complete disinterest in the opposite sex, for the most part the system still works.

Back in the Sixties, upwards of four hundred girls would proclaim themselves in season – now it is a quarter of that.

The principle reason is that it is too expensive these days for hard-pressed fathers to bring their daughters out; and the quality of girls who now attach themselves to the season has gone down. As an institution it is debased, but will continue to flourish while social mountaineers continue to don their climbing boots.

One major blow to the season came in the mid-Seventies when someone changed the tax laws on entertaining: up until that point, wise fathers used to claim their tax allowances for bringing their daughters out.

But the days when Viscount Bearstead gave a ball for a thousand of his daughter Felicity Samuel's closest friends are well and truly over. "Low-profile" is the clandestine word used now, a mixture of inverted snobbery, fear that hoodlums

57

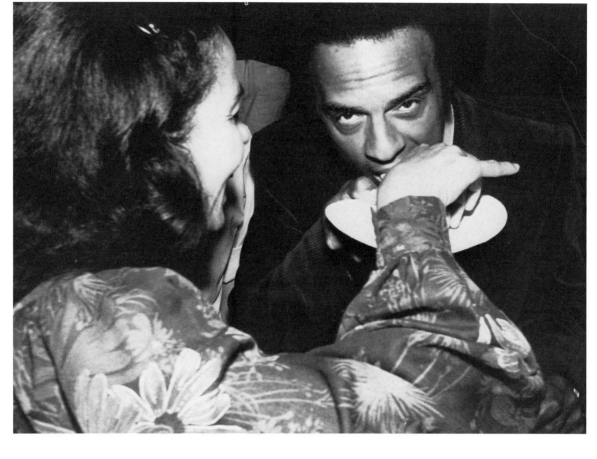

59

and the unemployed may turn up and wreck the joint and thanks that one is not forced to shell out too much money.

In fact, many a girl these days is being turned out into society on a combination of *méthode champenoise,* a succession of Laura Ashley dresses, and a short sharp shorthand course. The style has gone.

Now, too, is proclaimed an earnest attention to academism, or what passes for it amongst the upper set. The season these days is broken into two halves – before 'A' levels, and after. Since very few of these girls rise to the rank of Regius Professor, or indeed anything above the rank of secretary, it all seems a bit, one might say, academic.

Following the mother's lunches, where they all try to prove to each other that they came out, a series of tea-parties is arranged where the first tentative meetings of the girls take place. Occasionally a young blood is enticed along, but at this stage what matters is the girls getting to know each other, closing ranks and forming a tight bond that will last a lifetime.

At last the action gets going when the cocktail parties start in June (together with the *de rigueur* appearance at the Ascot royal meeting). For many girls, this will be their high point of personal entertaining, with the label of the chilled asti spumante carefully covered by the (hired) butler's napkin. Here girls will talk wistfully about having a dance in the autumn, and sketch airy pictures of entertaining three or four hundred. These are the girls who, towards the end of the

60

61

68

62

63

69

64

65

66

67

year, say they will be holding over their celebrations until the following year, go to everyone else's ball, and are never seen again.

Undoubtedly, there are still the show-offs who like to display their riches. A couple of years ago a proud mother, a South African, courted London society with a ball for her daughter at the Berkeley Hotel in Belgravia. A whole tree was flown in from her native country so that she could receive beneath it. It was not appreciated, particularly by those who could not afford to emulate such a gesture.

British society is so constructed that one can be desperately poor but acceptable, hideously rich and totally unacceptable. Breaking into the system is not impossible but defeats most contenders. The former try to secure their respectability through a "good" marriage to a wealthy, or at least titled, young man; and, of course, the season is dotted with broken women who have failed to achieve either of these things for their daughter.

Legend has it that one particularly ambitious mother used to listen on an intercom when her daughter brought young suitables home: if things were not going right, her voice would blare out of a speaker at the tenderest moments of passion. This particular girl tried hard to please her mother, and entertained three young earls in succession. However, such was her devotion that she would not relinquish her virtue until a proposal of marriage had been made. This girl, therefore, was condemned to perform a number of tricks worthy of the doxies of Shaftesbury Avenue in order to keep her young men happy. Needless to say, the

72

poor thing is still single. Many others have suffered similar fates.

Of course, some girls rise to be châtelaines of the grandest houses (their ideal goal). Others take a different course.

The classic case of the Deb Gone Wrong, which anxious mothers still lecture their little Arabellas with, is that of Jayne Harries, who ended up aged twenty-five in a Cranleigh public lavatory, dead from a drugs overdose. She had taken her first cocaine at a pre-season party when she was just fifteen. Jayne had been given £70,000 at her coming-out when she was seventeen. She left just £5676. It was said at the time she had died a victim of her father's social ambitions.

The playground of café society rarely shifts outside the square mile of Mayfair, bounded by Park Lane and Bond Street, Piccadilly and Oxford Street. New restaurants springing up may call for an expedition to Chelsea or, occasionally, Fulham: but those social mountaineers who come winging their way over Highgate Hill in their gold-mascoted Rolls-Royces soon discover that it is certain death to be seen entertaining, or being entertained, north of Oxford Street.

This theory, ludicrous though it may seem, was put to the acid test when restaurateur Nicky Kerman and others set up a nightclub called Dial 9 less than a minute's walk north of Oxford Street in Great Cumberland Place. Tastefully furnished, with professional staff, and headed up by the men who created the all-powerful Drones set: Michael Pearson (son of the unspeakably wealthy Lord Cowdray), Rupert Deen, John Bentley, Sir William Piggot-Brown and the like, it

71

had all the ingredients of success. Instead, the club became known as Dial 999 because, as one former member put it, "it was a disaster".

Others who have learnt from the geographical trick, though possibly for more complex reasons, include a carrot-haired Frenchwoman with indifferent manners who was welcomed into this world as Rachel Zylberberg. Her adoptive name is Regine and, until she descended on London in 1979, was considered to be the epitome of all that was best in café society. She had clubs in Paris and Monte Carlo, and a burgeoning nightclub empire across the world as she set up franchise operations in Rio and elsewhere.

She came to London and failed, because in the *bon mot* of Viscountess Rothermere: "This will never work – it's too far out of town."

For Regine had picked as the site for her club the old Derry and Tom's building in Kensington, a stone's throw from Kensington Palace but light years away from the rest of London's nightlife. Brazenly, she and the two men who founded the club, Nandkishore Ram and Gilbert Brown, opened up with a party whose guests included Princess Caroline of Monaco, who looked incredibly bored during the whole evening. It was not an auspicious start. Regine's hoped-for connection with our Royal Family did not work out – Prince Andrew was not allowed to go – and things turned ugly when the eminently civilized Belgian Ambassador, Robert Vaes, was thumped by a bouncer for getting too close to the puppet-state princess.

Only those with cash businesses did not find the prices audacious, and the

76

72

occasional parties thrown by Regine to show that she knew a lot of famous people were not, in the end, a success.

Sixteen months later, Regine quit, never having come to grips with London society and leaving behind a club that was veering towards bankruptcy. In May 1981 it crashed with a £1.1 million deficit.

Undoubtedly the best nightclub in London – its members say, in the world – is Annabel's in Berkeley Square. Unprepossessing from the outside – it is in the basement underneath the delightfully pretty Clermont gaming club – it is a nightmare inside. The layout is uncomfortable, it is too dark, and the braying of

74

76

young Guards officers in the bar can be unspeakable.

But the food is good, the service is impeccable, and the sense of mutual congratulation amongst the members – that they are there, and the rest of the world is outside, gloomily pressing its nose against the glass – is enough to buoy up one's feelings even after the astronomic bill is presented.

Gossip columnists are barred from Annabel's, which is why there have never been any stories about Prince Charles dancing the night away with a variety of married women. The place was named after the remarkable Lady Annabel Goldsmith, whose wedding to tycoon Sir James Goldsmith is described elsewhere in this book.

Many of the original crowd have moved on from Annabel's to other, even more exclusive clubs, usually started by Mark Birley, Lady Annabel's first husband. This minority of rich and powerful moguls rarely expose themselves to public gaze, but their absence was felt after they moved on, following the club being laconically retitled Arabel's after the mid-seventies influx of oil sheikhs.

Of the other clubs, Tramp in Jermyn Street stands out. In existence since some of its present patrons were in short trousers, it has achieved a much more informal clientele and at one stage was thought to have merged with Madame Tussaud's since the waxwork of George Best was permanently attached to one end of the bar. More sober members of Tramp would occasionally talk to the waxwork, and on a good night it would take a drink off them.

Tramp, too, took the policy early on that gossip columnists should not be allowed in, thus retaining their clientele for years as they felt they can go there and misbehave with relative safety. As with Annabel's, of course, the gossip columnists do get in, but tend to keep very quiet since they like to go back there themselves.

A lively attempt to rival Tramp was started early in 1981 on the opposite side of Piccadilly. Called Tokyo Joe's, it had the distinct advantage of Dai Llewellyn as its "greeter" and an excellent layout. Its gimmick was to have portraits of the famous on the walls, thinly disguised, in the obvious hope that these people would come to patronize the place.

An early disappointment for this idea came when Bianca Jagger strolled into the club with her current walker, one Olivier de Montal. De Montal's attention was drawn to the portrait of Bianca, which also featured Mick Jagger and his girlfriend, Jerry Hall. He ripped the oval-framed work from its mountings, threw it to the floor, and leapt up and down on it until it was no more.

Other gimmicks to draw in the loose-pursed often meet with similar disaster. Bennett, a club suffering the perennial geographical drawback by being sited in Battersea, had a flickering vogue just about the time when Roddy Llewellyn's relationship with Princess Margaret was at its height. Roddy had "done" the garden of the club, a pocket-handkerchief affair, and it was much hoped that his involvement with the place would bring royal patronage. It did not. Worse, few of London's true café society are familiar with the terrain south of the Thames and would continually find themselves heading towards Brighton, Eastbourne or Hastings after a night's carousal.

An early attempt to revive the place by glassing over the dance floor and putting piranha fish underneath somehow failed to capture the popular imagination, and the place has become a huge success, catering for those who have no social pretentions at all. Later the place changed its name, in gross bad taste, to "Riots".

Gambling clubs are a different scene altogether and attract an entirely different clientele. One of the grandest is Aspinall's, near Harrods, with one of London's finest chefs. Owned by zoo keeper John Aspinall, it probably represents the furthest he will go in gaming – although he recently bought the Curzon House Club in Mayfair for £250,000.

Its licence was not renewed. Aspinall brought style to gaming in London by opening the Clermont Club, which attracted a set including the missing Earl of Lucan. After a period when the place was swamped with visiting Arabs, it has started to regain its old clientele, such as the Earl of Carnarvon. The club is owned by *Playboy*.

The name 'Playboy' in London was for long synonymous with its figurehead, Victor Lownes III. Unlike his Chicago counterpart, Hugh Hefner, Lownes represented a red-blooded approach to women and to life.

The Playboy Club itself in Park Lane attracted a rich but not socially acceptable

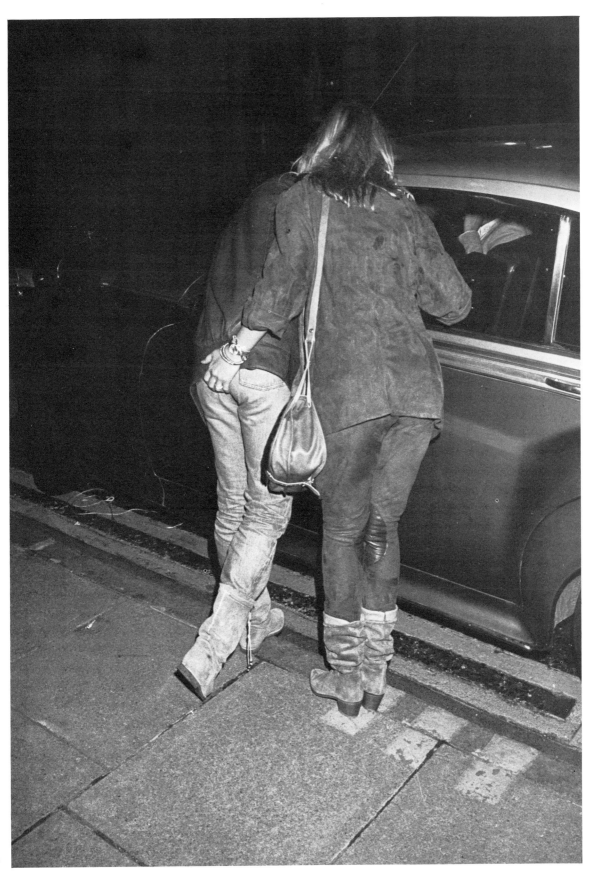

crowd, but Lownes's own personal contacts, reinforced by his lavish hospitality, his quick wit and attractive "aides", proved to be a different matter.

Lownes's country residence, Stocks, in Hertfordshire, became the focus of outrageous parties heavily covered by the press, entreés to which were much in demand. While Lownes remained blissfully unaware, scenes hardly short of Caligula took place in and around the grounds. One of the more revolting was the sight of a naked Reginald Bosanquet, wakened from his dreams by the merciless taunting of the *Daily Express*'s Peter Tory, and beside himself with rage.

Chicago-born Lownes acquired many English habits, such as riding to hounds, perhaps not realizing that true café society does not like to expose itself to the elements. Lownes's achievements – he became Britain's highest paid executive at £300,000 a year before his sacking in early 1981 – raised him above the level of social climber. But there are plenty of other folk who have set out without maps into the difficult waters of society.

One spectacular example was an Australian gambler called Peter Caplan, whose outrageous attempts at storming the walls of London society would have been described as pathetic, were they not so hilarious.

Introduced to professional party-giver Liz Brewer and Dai Llewellyn, Caplan told them: "I want to give the most talked-about party in town."

Since no one would go to a party given by an unknown Australian, however lavish, a suitable charity had to be found to disguise Caplan's ambitions, and the choice fell to Lord Oaksey's injured jockeys' fund. Llewellyn and Brewer were then employed at the fee of £3,000 to get suitable personalities to come, while Caplan invited his own chance acquaintances: taxi drivers, hall porters, hair-dressers and the like.

The party, held at Regine's cost £10,000. Its guests included Stirling Moss, Lord Weymouth, and Larry Adler.

Caplan, unsure of his guests and with the television team he had employed to film the event anxiously dogging his footsteps, curtly asked who Adler was. "That," said a tongue-in-cheek-guest, "is the greatest harmonica player in the world." This was enough for Caplan who then spent the rest of the evening introducing Adler to everyone as his old friend.

The party, and Caplan's naked ambition, drew hoots of derision from the two hundred and fifty guests and, after the universal ridicule delivered by the press, Caplan caught a plane back to Australia – having paid his bills – and was never seen again.

As one guest said as Caplan lowered his nose into actress Imogen Hassall's décolletage: "There is a man who has walked through society's revolving door . . . and out again – in one evening."

Hardly less audacious, though admittedly relatively more successful, have been the social ambitions of one Victor Melik, a leather merchant who burst onto the London scene in the Seventies. Undoubtedly rich, he first came into prominence having been introduced to the ubiquitous family Llewellyn after taking a cottage on their Llanfair estate.

Living high off the hog, Melik would use his private jet to entice gullible socialites to join him on weekend holidays on the Continent, and moved himself

79

80

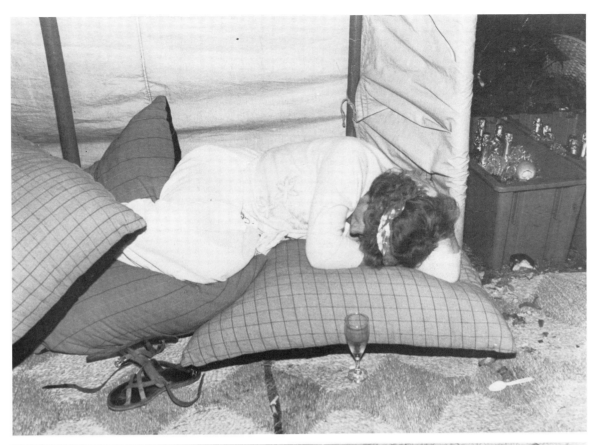

81

82

83

from a flat in Knightsbridge to a house off Eaton Square in Belgravia. Perhaps the high point of his social mountaineering came with a party for two hundred "friends" at Wedgie nightclub in Chelsea costing, some estimate, £10,000. It was said that Melik knew perhaps half of them.

Further evidence of extravagance for the benefit of future, as-yet-unknown, friends can be found at the Kensington door of Ken Lieberman who long ago was not so very well known, apart from being a successful businessman.

But in three successive years Lieberman changed all that by hosting a series of tennis parties which grew so large that he felt constrained to buy the house next door, then the house next door to *that* in order to be able to cope with the guests.

During a Cowboys-and-Indians fancy-dress party, a horse was actually spotted in the house along with guests Arthur Ashe, Ilie Nastase, John Lloyd, Andrew Young and others. It would not be true to say, however, that Lieberman always knew who was who: a friend was quoted as saying "He had six hundred guests last year and didn't know half of them".

But while the barriers are breaking down for those who wish to assail them, there is no absolute guarantee that social acceptability can be bought.

One particular hurdle which sorts out the men from the boy mountaineers is the

84

annual ritual of the Royal Ascot meeting. A far more élitist race-meeting than any other, the question of social acceptability stares you in the face as you enter the racecourse.

Those who have influence find themselves with little pasteboard badges upon their chests declaring that they are members of the Royal Enclosure (even more desirable: enclosure badges which have Royal Household printed on them). These can be got only if you know someone who has been a member of the Enclosure for the past four years, and many a would-be racegoer has decided to miss Ascot "this year" because no-one will sign them in.

In fact, the privilege only extends to having a decent view of the finish and getting a closer look at the Queen and her party. But there is no absolute guarantee that people will get in, just because they have found a sponsor. The Queen's representative, the Marquess of Abergavenny, quite openly states that a blacklist operates at Ascot to keep out undesirables: "I don't want it looking like Blackpool beach." In fact the rules, unwritten, are: no debtors, no rotters. Unfortunately the second rule hardly applies any more.

Some say that since the doors of the Enclosure were opened to the ludicrous and vainly self-publicizing Mrs Gertrude Shilling, whose son is a successful hatter but

whose own headgear arrangements at the annual meeting are greeted with universal horror, another sort of person has arrived in the hallowed area. Once more, they say, the barricades are crumbling: once more the *vieux pauvres* take a backward step from the insidious advances of the *nouveaux riches*.

Café society, naturally enough, has to have its café. And no matter where else everyone goes, they all, at some stage or another, end up in the establishment just off Piccadilly, presided over by Irish drunk Peter Langan.

It is called Langan's Brasserie, and serves over-rich food to over-rich clients.

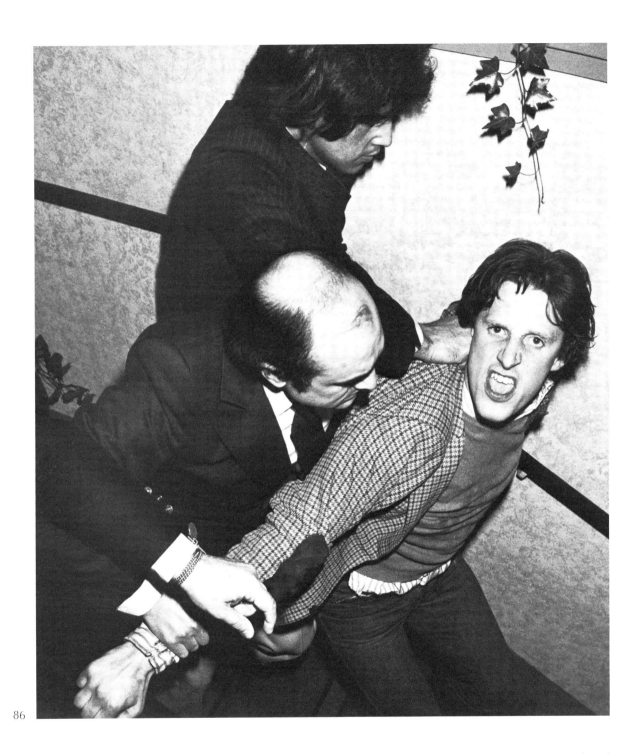

86

Langan, the son of an Eire oil executive, drinks annually £40,000 worth of champagne, insults his customers, and does his best to drive everybody away. Some keep their promises never to return: most forget them as soon as they forget their swingeing bill.

In any event, it is the one restaurant in London where, any time of the day or night, you will find the up-and-coming doing their best to rub shoulders with those who have already upped and come.

Once, Langan was confronted by an irate customer who had unfortunately

found a dead cockroach (was the food *that* poisonous?) in the ladies' powder room. She brought it out, horrified, and waggled it by one of its legs under Langan's nose.

"What do you intend to do about *this*?" she shrieked.

Langan promptly swallowed the insect with a glass of vintage Krug.

That was on one of his more gentlemanly nights. On another occasion he took exception to a dog brought in by Italian designer Elio Fiorucci. He got down and crawled between the table legs in the restaurant, and bit the beast on its hindquarters.

Human beings hardly get away with better treatment. Toothy Lady Falkender, together with a highly nervous Janet Street Porter, were forced to hide in the ladies' loo after Langan threatened them with a certain sexual act that neither of them was in the mood for just at that moment.

Of course, Langan's intake of champagne tends to be a bit on the high side: at one stage it was up to twelve bottles a day.

Indeed, champagne is all-purpose at Langan's. Once the kitchen caught fire, and was kept under control until the fire brigade arrived with constant dousings of champers, while patrons were given consoling glasses of it out on the pavement. On a golfing trip to Portugal, Langan cleaned out the hotel by ordering seventy bottles of champagne, propositioned a nun and two air hostesses on the flight back, and tore his shirt to shreds giving each of the passengers a memento.

88

89

90

91

The oceans of free champagne would mean nothing, were not someone there to report that it had been bought and consumed – which is where the gossip columnists come in.

Fleet Street's gossip columnists are a rough-and-ready lot, generally disaffected former public schoolboys whose social ambitions run higher than their status would otherwise allow. They are snobs. They take intense delight in striking attitudes in print which they would never dare repeat around their own dinner-tables for fear of ridicule.

They can turn rising stars into tear-stained no-hopers just by an ill-considered (come to that, well considered) phrase. Indeed, their power can go far beyond that of other journalists.

It is generally held in Fleet Street that gossip columnists were responsible, unwittingly perhaps, for the tragic death of starlet Imogen Hassall, who committed suicide as her career fell in tatters around her.

"You don't write about me any more – you shit," she told one columnist,

genuinely disappointed because he was disinclined to write about her latest stage play at Watford.

The poor girl suffered a history of gynaecological mishaps and after each would rise from her anaesthetic to call a columnist somewhere in Fleet Street to render a blow-by-blow account of her latest trouble.

In the end, Imogen Hassall was a name that would raise a howl of laughter in the journalists' watering-hole, El Vino's; no one would write about her any more. And, bereft of new headlines to stick in her scrapbook, Imogen took her life, poor thing. They wrote about her then.

There are two principal columns in Fleet Street: Nigel Dempster's *Daily Mail* Diary, and the *Daily Express's* William Hickey column.

Hickey is run by the patrician son of a diplomat and former Royal Shakespeare Company actor, Peter Tory. He has a staff of four reporters. Dempster's column, despite its focus on the individual, also has a staff of reporters.

94

In the late Seventies, gossip had become a revived trade. For years it was in the doldrums after the Press Council had been set up, and the excesses of some of the more adventurous columns of the late Fifties had been curbed.

Dempster, and later Peter McKay who now runs a gossip column on the *Daily Mirror*, revived the art and put back the bitch. Pathetic attempts by other newspapers – the *Sun*, the *News of the World*, the *Daily Star* – to start gossip columns have failed abysmally. This is principally because on these downmarket newspapers they do not employ ex-public schoolboys, and beer scriveners from Glasgow do not go down well in the Ritz.

Dempster it is, however, who stands out head and shoulders above the rest of the hacks, as they like to call themselves. This sleek, muscular figure brings both fear and joy into the hearts of London's society hostesses.

A party with "Nigel" present (the surname is discarded) can be counted a success, even if hardly anyone else turns up.

95

Dempster has got to this not wholly enviable position by years of sheer hard work and obsessive devotion to his job. In every gossip columnist there has to be an element of the social climber, and Nigel's early years on the rival "Hickey" page gave full rein to his fantasies.

Now he is a part of that Establishment under which he once sought to put a banana-skin – or almost. He is a complex Jekyll-and-Hyde figure with a high rating of unpredictability. Occasionally the unpredictability will take an alarming turn, as on the day he had a spectacular fight at the Derby, his adversary having to flee by helicopter once they had been parted.

On another occasion, he brought a party given by journalists of Times Newspapers – about to go off the streets for a year – grinding to a halt, no mean feat. He and left-wing writer Christopher Hitchens were fighting.

99

But there is another side to his character; he is one of the most generous, amiable and best-informed men in his sphere and, unlike most other gossip columnists, actually knows the people he writes about.

The man whom Dempster succeeded as editor of the *Mail* Diary, who then went on to the *Daily Mirror*, was someone called Paul Callan. Callan is worthy of note to illustrate the fantasy world the gossipers sink into, with their expense accounts, their endless champagne and free dinners. For twenty years in Fleet Street, Callan convinced everyone that he was an Old Etonian – a remarkable feat, given that journalists tend to be inquistive souls and like to know every detail about their colleagues.

Callan was finally unfrocked by a justified, but as usual tasteless, exposé in *Private Eye*. He had been to South Norwood Secondary Modern School. But his lengthy fantasy proved one thing: all gossip columnists wish they had been to Eton. Even Dempster used to wear the black-and-blue O E tie.

One person who did actually go there is the man the hacks, above all others, love to hate. He is financier and grocer Sir James Goldsmith.

Jimmy's days as a Mayfair playboy have been replaced by a dedication to building an empire some say he hopes to make as big as the Holy Roman. This kind of single-mindedness is known to sway the objectivity of all sorts of men, and Jimmy is no exception.

When he went to speak the valediction on his ill-fated *Now!* magazine,

100

101

103

102

103

104

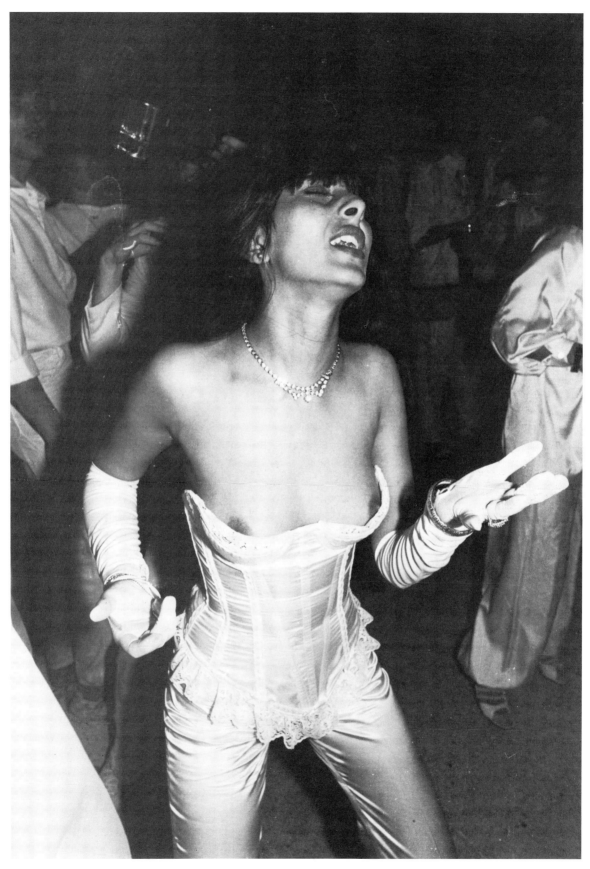

Goldsmith took a hefty retinue along, just in case things turned nasty. Decoy cars were laid on for him, and though he was speaking to mild-mannered journalists rather than belligerent printers he had anticipated the worst.

Violence even spilled over on his wedding day when he married the former Lady Annabel Birley in Paris. An *Express* photographer, Bill Lovelace, tried to take pictures of the couple in the street. Goldsmith called for a couple of henchmen and together they bundled Lovelace into the premises of Générale Occidentale, his French holding company. Lovelace was given a drubbing, breaking his glasses and camera and bruising his ribs, while Goldsmith made his escape.

Jimmy, undismayed at having a set-to even on his wedding day, then wrote a crowing letter to *The Times* bragging about what he had done.

If Jimmy Goldsmith is an untypical product of Eton, so too is one David St Vincent Llewellyn, more commonly known as Dai.

For some extraordinary reason Llewellyn, the son of a Welsh baronet whose forebear is said to have bought the title from Lloyd George, has come to represent the archetypal playboy: the other kind of unemployed, the champagne guzzling, Gucci-heeled layabout who is welcomed by a thousand open doors in Mayfair.

In fact this vision was, at one stage, true in part. Llewellyn first came to prominence in the early Seventies when he operated the door at the Clermont Club in Berkeley Square. He wore a passable dinner jacket and vulgar high-heeled patent shoes, but the undeniable charm, the raffish good-humour, and his encyclopaedic knowledge of faces and personalities which, in other circumstances, would have made him a sure-fire hit as the owner of a stately home was then at its height.

It was then the high-point of his playboy days, when he and one Nigel Pollitzer had just come back from Paris, boasting they had been driving Princess Caroline of Monaco around in a car while both made unsuccessful attempts at suborning her.

Llewellyn's subsequent successes have been mainly of the printed word: a succession of "life stories" has appeared in popular newspapers, outlining the minutiae of his life and that of his brother, Roddy. London excitedly felt that he had gone too far when he revealed rather boring details of Roddy's relationship with Princess Margaret; but being the remarkable showman that he is, Llewellyn pulled back from the brink by marrying into the family of the Duke of Norfolk, Britain's premier peer. It was a rather bizarre occasion, with the scions of one of Britain's most ancient families on one side of the church balefully looking at the likes of Diana Dors, leather merchant Victor Melik, and other assorted bodies on the other.

What remains is, of course, an extraordinary man. Friends like him because his way of life seems dangerous: more jobs than the days in the year; extraordinary business associates. But the stamina with which he can down champagne appears not to diminish with his increasing girth and receding hairline.

London these days is woefully short of stars. Stars of the Fifties, like Douglas Fairbanks Jr, or the Dockers, or Nubar Gulbenkian, have faded away and never been replaced. Hostesses are often stuck as to where to find a personality to add gloss to their party.

Society is flattening out and certainly such film stars as we have do not care to go about looking glamorous any more.

Glenda Jackson, our greatest Oscar winner, would not be seen dead stepping out of a limousine, sequinned dress aglitter, and plunging into the latest nightclub. Ditto Julie Christie, ditto Vanessa Redgrave.

Hostesses have some hopes with Susannah York, but here some of the worst elements of Hollywood "style" can creep in. Confronted with cameras, she is likely to disappear behind high coat collars: no good for the paparazzi, so no good for the hostess.

Greater luck can be had with small-screen stars and, though both preserve an outer *froideur*, Angela Rippon and Anna Ford have both made themselves available for engagements. In Angela's case it is a natural progression from the early, mad, days when she was idolised but did not get about much: now she is a star of the Mark Macormack stable, established and relaxed socially.

Things are different with Anna. For a long time she appeared to be one of the most unhappy women around, with a patchy love-life and a basic incompatibility with her position. She expected her small-screen stardom to be switched on and off when she chose and resented publicity if it did not suit her : a naive, if occasionally touching, attitude. Her association with Mark Boxer, the immensely talented cartoonist and publisher, has brought happiness to all.

One of our other few stars around is the delectable caretaker's daughter, Lesley Anne Down, who in true café society style spent ten years with one boyfriend, then promptly married another. She then wed the mournful-looking Henri Gabriel – and subsequently dumped him.

With this dearth of home-grown talent to fill out the parties and receptions, one has to look further afield. And for a time the most prominent partygoer in this category was Britt Ekland, former wife of Peter Sellers.

Britt, who made £250,000 from a rather squalid set of memoirs, gave pop singer Rod Stewart all sorts of airs and graces above his station during their relationship. Since Rod's marriage to Alana Hamilton, it is fair to say the poor boy has calmed down now, but Miss Ekland has gone from strength to strength and man to man with alacrity. Her favourites in London included a group of youngsters who are peculiarly called "toy-boys".

One of the most fascinating girls around town is Susan George who, despite a long-standing relationship with Derek Webster, had previously managed to find time to accompany more men around town than would be deemed possible by one young lady. Jack Jones, Andy Gibb, Jimmy Connors, Guy McElwaine, Rod Stewart, Robert Winsor, Patrick Wayne, Henry Wynberg, John Lloyd, James Vaughan, John Leveson, Gerald Carroll, George Best, Benny Thomas, Tony Monopoly, to name but a lot. Apart from being raped in *Straw Dogs* and *Mandingo*, her claim to immortality is her relationship with Prince Charles.

Since then she has never looked back.

Some of the relationships which café society throws up are interesting indeed. Despite its legality, homosexuality is still treated with reserve in some quarters, and any number of socialites still hide their sexual preferences. As may be imagined, members of the House of Lords, cabinet ministers and others in public life can be just as queer as the more outrageous show-business entertainers who make their campness a trade-mark. But they tend towards a conventional front, often with marriages and children to bolster up their image. Indeed, some rue the day that Roy Jenkins turned homosexuality legitimate, since a major part of the fun of it – its clandestine nature – was wiped away for good.

In fact, the increasing blatancy of young men "coming out" hit an all-time high at the time when the Embassy Club, once the spiritual home of the Duke of Windsor and his set in pre-war years, re-opened in the late Seventies. Waiters were dressed in satin boxer shorts and little else, and the club's figurehead, called Stephen Hayter, dubbed himself in a rare moment of humour "Queen of the Night" – a phrase stolen from the carrot-haired Regine.

It seemed that everyone then discovered they had homosexual tendencies, and so excited was London by this new foible that there were a great number of (later rued) dalliances. The Embassy flourished, and other clubs started up in opposition, trying to trump them by operating such devices as barring women altogether – something the Embassy had the good sense to avoid.

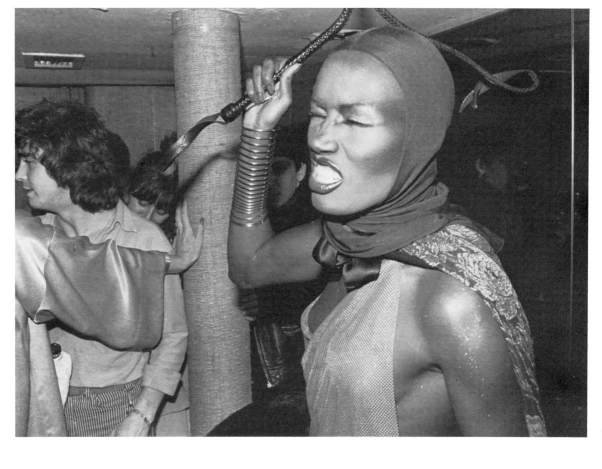

Other clubs, such as Legends just round the corner from the Old Bond Street premises of the Embassy, took a softer approach and while a large percentage of their clientele, mainly drawn from the show-business and rock worlds, was homosexual they labelled themselves "bisexual" clubs.

But while all this activity was going on, very few prominent society members would own up to being gay outside their own circle. One senior Member of Parliament, well known for his sexual preferences, summed it up to me thus: "I have never made a secret of it to those who I think will not be offended. To those who will be offended, I see no reason why I should go out of my way to upset them."

To a large degree, gossip writers and other journalists go along with this dual standard, largely because the libel laws in this country are so heavily weighted in favour of the litigant that a notorious pansy could easily bring an action against a newspaper for calling him queer – and get away with it.

Thus only hints are dropped about male sexual preferences in the gossip columns, leaving the reader to make up his own mind. More difficult still, from the gossip writers' point of view, is labelling the bisexuals and trying to pinpoint their relationships. A prime example was the wedding of someone close to certain members of the Royal Family; a notable absentee from the ceremony was the man who had enjoyed a sexual liaison, at different times, with both bride and groom. The best story the gossip columns could have all year – and yet they could only hint at it.

114

115

116

They turn instead to other unorthodox relationships which are more easily observed and less likely to collect a writ. Outstanding among these have been the still unusual pairings of aristocratic girls with black men – still, believe it or not, considered scandalous.

Both Viscountess Royston and Lady Carina FitzAlan Howard fell for black men. Both the men, ironically, were called Charles. Virginia Royston, the widow of Viscount Royston and mother of the Earl of Hardwicke, met a barman called Basil Charles while on holiday in Mustique in the mid-Seventies. They now share a house together on the island, happily living out of wedlock.

Lady Carina FitzAlan Howard, whose father the Duke of Norfolk is hereditary Earl Marshal, fell for a black club-owner called Noel Charles who ran an establishment in Barbados. The couple lived together for some time – to the undoubted embarrassment and shame of the Duke, a devout Roman Catholic. He refused to have Charles in the house, or recognise their relationship. In the end Carina, determined not to hurt the family name despite her deep feelings for him, chose to end the relationship and return to the family fold.

Another, less long-lasting union of this nature was between the ubiquitous Chantal d'Orthez and the black soul singer, Marvin Gaye. Possibly through fear of parental disapproval – her father is champagne magnate Vicomte d'Orthez and mother is actress Moira Lister – the liaison was a short one, and one which

surprisingly Chantal was not happy to have blazened from the rooftops.

Another member of the Norfolk family, Lady Anne FitzAlan Howard (more properly titled Baroness Herries) is one of the four daughters of the previous Duke, who died without producing a son. She took under her wing the unlikely figure of England cricketer Colin Cowdray, who left his wife Penny to move into her house on the Arundel Castle estate. What made this liaison particularly interesting was the late blossoming of the love affair: he is forty-eight, she is forty-three.

And whilst talking of extramarital linkages, no review would be complete without reference to Sir Maxwell Joseph, the multimillionaire head of a catering and hotels chain who created much bated breath when he was knighted in the 1981 New Year's Honours. For the woman by his side these past twenty years, though called Mrs Joseph, was not his wife. That privilege fell to Mrs *Sybil* Joseph, to whom he had been married for forty years. Upon his knighthood, Sybil naturally became Lady Joseph. But what of the woman in Max's life, *Eileen*? She had already changed her name by deed poll to Mrs Joseph. Was she now to be the first person to take a title by deed poll as well? Happily, Max solved the whole thing by starting divorce proceedings against Sybil and marrying Eileen. One knighthood had produced *two* Lady Josephs!

Where are the heirs to ancient titles which anxious mothers so desperately want for their daughters?

Well, there is Lord Burghersh, the man who preceded Dai Llewellyn as the greeter

120

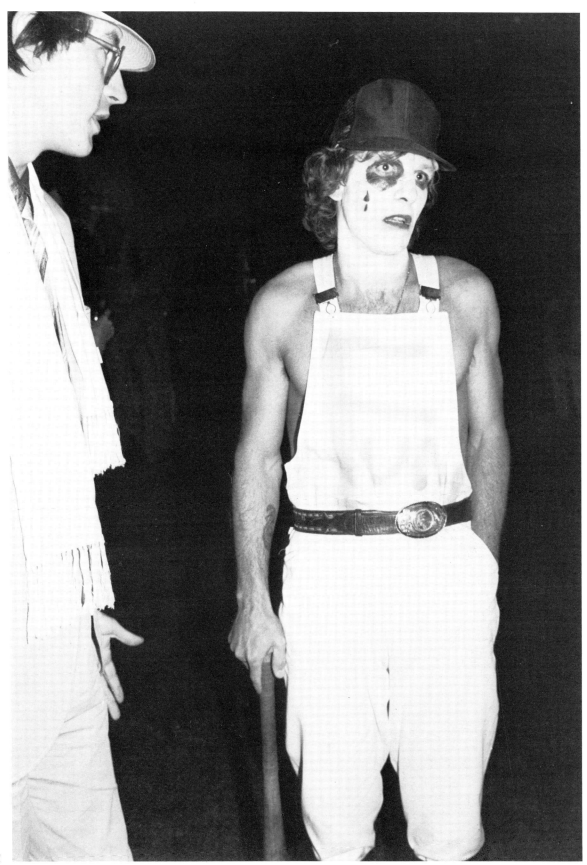

for Wedgies. Bobsleighing Burghie, whose father, the Earl of Westmorland, is Master of the Queen's Horse, was gently dissuaded from continuing this rather common form of employment and slipped into the delicate backwaters of Fine Art. But party-loving would-be brides should not give up hope. Parrot-interviewing Burghie still nurses secret ambitions of becoming another Regine.

There is the Marquess of Blandford, the heir to the Duke of Marlborough, who embarrassed his family by being rejected by the Army (his forebear being the brilliant general John Churchill). Jamie is a fun-loving sort, given to model-girls as well as those of high birth, and should therefore be looked at by a broader range of ambitious mums. After all, there is one of the most beautiful houses in England – Blenheim Palace – and 12,000 acres at stake.

And despite the fact that he is married and forty-nine, one can include in this category Viscount Weymouth, the deliciously dotty heir to Longleat and thousands of Wessex acres. He can be included because girlfriend after girlfriend approaches his "open" marriage to the Viscountess, actress Anna Gael, with haughty self-confidence. They go and look over Longleat, examine the Kama Sutra murals, and proclaim themselves satisfied with their surroundings, confident they can induce him into further marital arrangements. So far, no one has yet convinced this permanent teenager that it's a workable idea.

Café society is riddled with the PRs who push their products, their personalities and themselves to an alarming degree. It is they who throw the most lavish parties, they who know better than the gossip columnists who's in and who's out. In fact, it is from them that much of the information comes which appears in the columns, one way or the other. Standing head and shoulders above the lot is Denise, Lady Kilmarnock, a terrifying woman who few but the tallest can look squarely in the eye. Hers is not the business of consorting with the columnists, but with fixing upper-notch entertainments. She once said she had considered having an operation to lower her *tailleur*. "But I thought when I had been cut down my arms would have swung by me like an ape's."

Here, then, is a modest reflection of a heterogeneous and totally unpredictable social grouping which anthropologists of future generations will try, one suspects without success, to pinpoint. Put another way, you don't know who's going to be flavour of the month next.

Fashions swing this way and that, and with them the fortunes of the socially ambitious. One day you're in, the next day you're out. It's the nearest one can get to Andy Warhol's dictum that each person should be famous for fifteen minutes.

For an outsider, entry into this terrifying group can be more than their sanity is worth. But once inside looking out, it can give the most wonderfully warm sensations of satisfaction, of élitism, of being bullet-proof.

Reconstructed in the way that it is in the Eighties, café society in its present form will last until the end of the century, but the components will change. The old aristocracy will withdraw, and a society based more on New York than on Paris will take its place.

In the meantime, there is fun to be had. There is glamour to be had. There is the delicious expectation, every morning from now until forever, of waiting for that satisfying plop on the doormat as the envelopes come flooding through, each containing those passports to paradise, engraved "By Invitation Only".

Index to photographs